Editor
Eric Migliaccio

Managing Editor
Ina Massler Levin, M.A.

Cover Artist
Marilyn Goldberg

Art Production Manager
Kevin Barnes

Imaging
Rosa C. See

Publisher
Mary D. Smith, M.S. Ed.

Crossword Puzzles

Grades 3-4

Author

Michael H. Levin, M.A., N.B.C.T.

Teacher Created Resources, Inc.
6421 Industry Way
Westminster, CA 92683
www.teachercreated.com
ISBN-1-4206-5997-9
©2006 Teacher Created Resources, Inc.
Made in U.S.A.

Table of Contents

Introduction

Kids and puzzles just seem to go together. Kids love to figure puzzles out; and while they're using their positive brain energy, they are reinforcing many of the concepts we hope they will learn. In this series, we have concentrated on two of their favorites: crossword puzzles and word searches. They have been developed for the primary grades where concentration and mental dexterity need constant practice.

You will find 52 crossword puzzles on the following pages that will delight your students on a variety of subjects. Although easier than the crossword puzzles found in the daily newspaper, they have the same across-and-down format. They are designed to challenge your students but not frustrate them.

Your students will enjoy finding the words, of course. However, these puzzles were also designed to allow you to further use them in your course of study. There are puzzles that will reinforce the language, math, social studies, and science skills that you are already teaching. These puzzles can aid you in your curriculum or be a starting point for oral and written reports. For example, if you assign each of your students the name of a landmark found in the puzzle on page 32, you can have them research it and explain to the class its importance.

Having students create their own crossword puzzles would reinforce and further their understanding of the subject. As you move through the year and their multiplication skills become more advanced, why not have your students create a puzzle that reflects their newly acquired knowledge? Perhaps you have a student fascinated by space exploration. Instead of using the names of world explorers found on page 17, the student can create a puzzle using the names of astronauts. On page 51, you will find familiar pairs. As a group assignment, your students will enjoy coming up with their own list of pairs and making a puzzle that will challenge the other members of the class.

We hope these puzzles provide hours of enjoyment for your class. We know you'll be adding your own ideas about how to use them. Have fun!

Abbreviations

Use the clues below to fill in the puzzle with the long form of the abbreviations given below.

Across

1. M.D.
4. esp.
6. st.
11. FYI
13. I.O.U.

Down

2. COD
3. ASAP
5. mph
7. bldg.
8. P.O.
9. lbs.
10. RR
12. oz. (*plural*)

Addition

Use the clues below to fill in the puzzle with number words.

Across

4. four plus five plus one
6. twenty-two plus eighteen
8. twenty plus six plus thirteen
10. fourteen plus six plus four
12. seven plus two plus ten
13. twenty-six plus twenty-three
14. fourteen plus eighteen

Down

1. fifteen plus twenty
2. eight plus four plus eight
3. seven plus five plus five
5. twenty plus thirty
8. twenty-two plus sixteen
9. seventeen plus twelve
11. twenty plus twenty-six

         #5997 Start to Finish: Crossword Puzzles

All Things Being Equal

Use the clues below to fill in the puzzle with number words.

Across

2. 1 ton = 2,000 _____

5. 1 pint = 2 _____

7. 1 quarter = 25 _____

9. 1 foot = 12 _____

11. 1 month = 4 _____

12. 1 meter = 3.3 _____

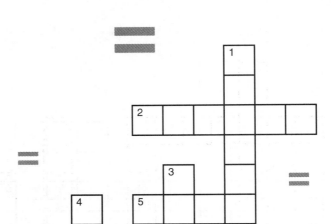

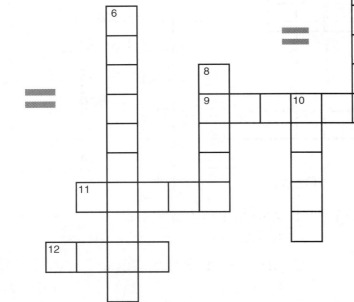

Down

1. 1 year = 12 _____

3. 1 gallon = 4 _____

4. 1 cup = 8 _____

6. 1 inch = 2.54 _____

8. 1 quart = 2 _____

10. 1 day = 24 _____

Analogies

An *analogy* is a way to compare things. Use the Word Box to help you complete the analogies below. Write your answers in the crossword puzzle.

Word Box

belt

house

curtain

bird

niece

head

December

library

hungry

captain

ceiling

Across

2. window is to _____ as floor is to rug

6. ship is to _____ as airplane is to pilot

7. eat is to _____ as sleep is to tired

8. shoe is to foot as hat is to _____

9. November is to Thanksgiving as _____ is to Christmas

Down

1. zoo is to animals as _____ is to books

2. floor is to bottom as _____ is to top

3. _____ is to aunt as nephew is to uncle

4. _____ is to waist as bracelet is to wrist

5. _____ is to nest as bee is to hive

8. gate is to yard as door is to _____

Antonyms 1

An *antonym* is an opposite. Fill in the puzzle with antonyms of the clues below.

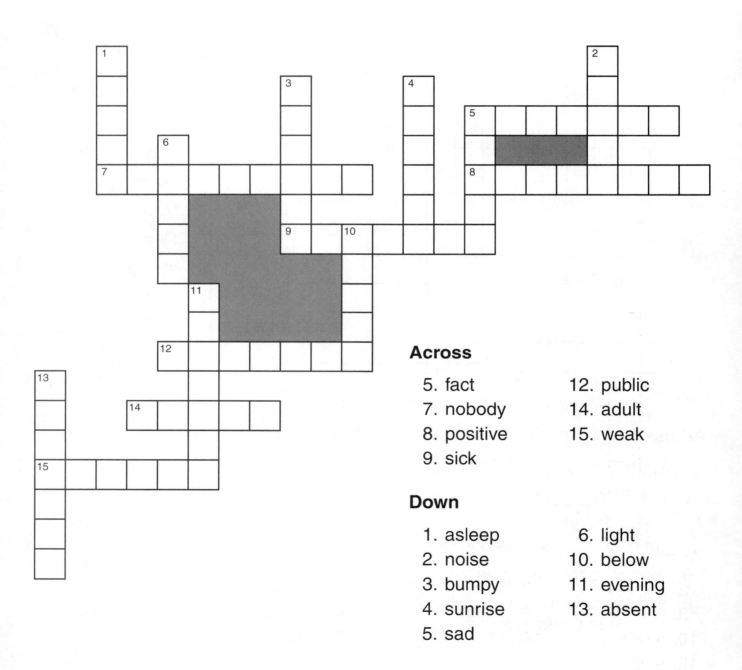

Across

5. fact
7. nobody
8. positive
9. sick

12. public
14. adult
15. weak

Down

1. asleep
2. noise
3. bumpy
4. sunrise
5. sad

6. light
10. below
11. evening
13. absent

Antonyms 2

An *antonym* is an opposite. Fill in the puzzle with antonyms of the clues below.

Across

2. answer
3. full
10. modern
12. easy
13. hero
15. guilty
16. top

Down

1. forget
4. student
5. here
6. forward
7. slow
8. release
9. crooked
11. married
14. tame

Birthstones

Each month of the year has its own birthstone. Write in the months that match the birthstones below.

Across

1. topaz
4. pearl
6. turquoise
8. sardonyx
9. garnet
10. emerald
11. diamond

Down

2. opal
3. amethyst
5. sapphire
7. ruby
10. aquamarine

Capitals

Name the state or province that goes with each of the capitals listed below. Use the Word Box to help you.

Word Box

New York
Virginia
Quebec
Manitoba
British Columbia
Wyoming
Iowa
Texas
Georgia
Utah
Missouri
Ontario
California
Alberta
Colorado
Louisiana

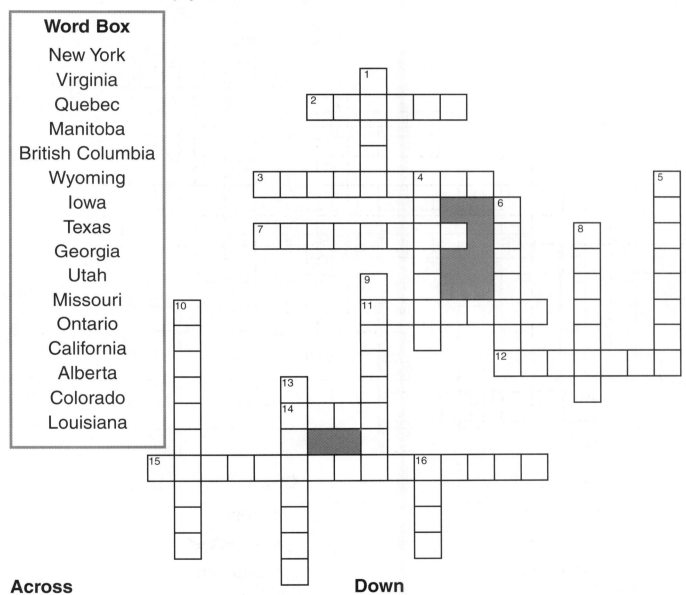

Across

2. Ottowa
3. Baton Rouge
7. Winnipeg
11. Toronto
12. Atlanta
14. Des Moines
15. Victoria

Down

1. Austin
4. Edmonton
5. Richmond
6. Cheyenne
8. Albany
9. Denver
10. Sacramento
13. Jefferson City
16. Salt Lake City

Complete It 1

The clues given below are the shortened forms of words. Write the full word in the puzzle. Example: *photo* is the shortened form of *photograph*.

Across

2. phone
3. burger
6. ref
7. gym
10. tux
11. taxi
13. auto
15. vet
16. plane
17. exam
18. gas

Down

1. fridge
4. specs
5. limo
8. sub
9. bike
12. math
14. champ

Complete It 2

The clues given below are the shortened forms of words. Write the full word in the puzzle. Example: *phone* is the shortened form of *telephone*.

Across

1. flu
6. photo
7. exam
8. copter
10. ad
11. lab

Down

2. tie
3. teen
4. mod
5. movie
6. prof
9. fan

Compound Words

Use the clues and the Word Box below to fill in the puzzle with compound words.

Across

2. used to tell time
6. no shoes
8. to walk quietly
9. lifted to let large ships pass
10. small-sized dessert with frosting
11. used to see
12. worn with slippers in the morning

Down

1. baseball position
3. a hair style worn by people with long hair
4. a tall building
5. tools used to make things
7. worn over clothes to keep them clean
8. used to guide large ships into port

Word Box

barefoot
bathrobe
cupcake
drawbridge
eyeball
hardware
outfield
overalls
ponytail
skyscraper
tiptoe
tugboat
wristwatch

Computer Terms

Use the Word Box and the clues below to help you fill in the puzzle with computer terms.

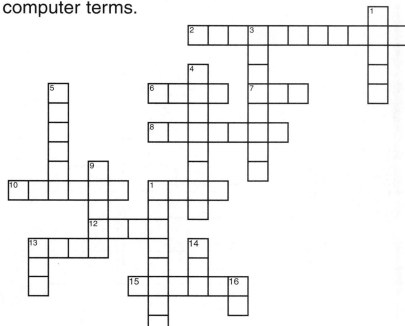

Word Box

byte	hacker
net	download
laptop	motherboard
spam	bug
crash	PC
cursor	monitor
icon	mouse
DVD	hardcopy
surf	software

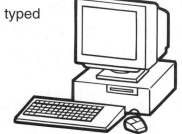

Across

2. a computer's main circuit board
6. a small image on the screen that represents an object or application
7. abbreviation for "digital video disc"
8. display screen on which the computer images can be seen
10. a blinking character that shows where keystrokes will appear when typed
11. e-mail that has not been asked for
12. a sports term that means "to browse around the Internet"
13. a unit of data, almost always consisting of 8 bits
15. small, portable computer designed for use during travel

Down

1. can result in the loss of all unsaved data
3. printed output on paper, film, or other permanent medium
4. to transfer a copy of something from a remote computer to your computer
5. a person who uses computer knowledge to illegally obtain information from another computer
9. common pointing device that has a flat-bottom and is designed to be used with one hand
11. computer programs that make hardware work
13. a recurring problem that prevents a system from working properly
14. short for "Internet"
16. short for "personal computer"

Division

Use the clues below to fill in the puzzle with number words.

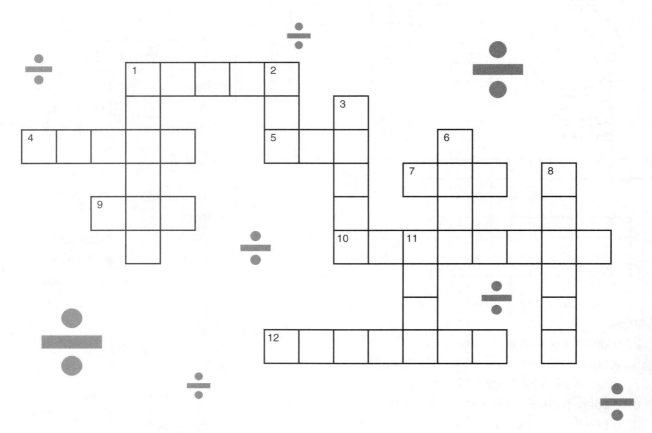

Across

1. twenty-four divided by three
4. twelve divided by four
5. nine divided by nine
7. eighteen divided by three
9. twenty divided by two
10. nineteen divided by one
12. thirty divided by two

Down

1. twenty-two divided by two
2. twelve divided by six
3. twenty-eight divided by four
6. twenty-five divided by five
8. thirty-six divided by three
11. thirty-six divided by four

Explorers

Use the clues to fill in the puzzle with the names of famous explorers.

Across

2. Spanish; explored and named Florida (1497)

6. French; explored the course of St. Lawrence River and the northeastern United States (1539)

8. Spanish; explored and conquered Mexico (1519)

9. Spanish; explored Panama and reached the Pacific Ocean (1513)

10. Portuguese; began an expedition that went around the world (1519)

Down

1. Italian; sailed four times from Spain to America (1492)

3. Italian; traveled to India and China (1271)

4. Norse; explored Canada and New England (1000)

5. Portuguese; sailed around the Cape of Hope to India (1504)

6. Spanish; explored southeastern U.S. (1519)

7. English; explored areas in northern U.S. and eastern Canada. Has a river and a bay named after him (1609)

Finish the Group

Each of the group of words below forms a group—but something is missing! Fill in the missing word or name in the puzzle.

Across

2. what, when, why, how, who, _____

4. Superior, Michigan, Erie, Ontario, _____

5. Mama Bear, Papa Bear, _____

7. blue, red, yellow, orange, green, violet, _____

9. Earth, Uranus, Pluto, Mercury, Mars, Saturn, Jupiter, Neptune, _____

10. quarter, nickel, penny, dime, _____

11. November, April, June, _____

12. sight, hearing, taste, smell, _____

Down

1. red, blue, _____

3. George Washington, Abraham Lincoln, Theodore Roosevelt, _____

6. North America, Europe, Antarctica, Australia, South America, Africa, _____

8. addition, subtraction, multiplication, _____

Fruits

Use the clues below to fill in the puzzle with the names of fruits.

Across

3. green or purple; wine is made from them
6. yellow and sour
8. same as its color; make juice from it
9. small and red
10. yellow or orange; usually is more tart than sweet
11. red; most people think its a vegetable; used in a salad

Down

1. give it to your teacher
2. sweet; red; with a green stem on top
4. grows in a palm tree; very hard shell
5. large; green on the outside and red with many pits on the inside; very sweet
7. yellow and long

Halloween

Use the clues below to fill in the puzzle with Halloween words.

Across

2. what we say on Halloween when we come to someone's door
5. an orange Halloween squash
6. the character we are when dressed in a sheet
8. this pretend man is filled with hay
11. a scary, carved pumpkin

Down

1. the animal we think about during Halloween
3. the Halloween color (along with black)
4. a character who rides on a broomstick
7. the month Halloween is found
9. the treat we hope to get
10. the season Halloween is found
12. the time of day when we trick or treat

Homographs 1

A *homograph* is a word that is written the same as another word but has a different meaning. Use the Word Box and clues to complete the puzzle.

Word Box				
match	bear	hold	content	bat
chop	bill	batter	might	hatch
light	cobbler	lock	bridge	chow

Across

2. breed of dog/slang for "food"
4. baseball player/liquid measure used for cakes
5. club/flying animal
8. large animal/to carry or support
9. bring forth young from an egg/opening in a ship's deck
10. past tense of "may"/power
12. not heavy/not dark

Down

1. fasten door/curl of hair
2. all things inside/satisfied
3. one who fixes shoes/fruit pie with one crust
5. a way over a river/card game
6. stick used to light fires/equal
7. cut of meat/slicing motion
8. statement of money owed/beak
11. grasp/part of a ship

Homographs 2

A *homograph* is a word that is written the same as another word but has a different meaning. Use the Word Box and clues to complete the puzzle.

Word Box					
pool	spell	meter	ring	rare	scale
pop	jerky	pupil	long	pitcher	ruler

Across

3. unit of length/device that keeps track of something
5. tool for measuring weight/outer layer of fish or snakes
6. circle/bell sound
7. tank with water/game played with balls on a table
8. opposite of short/wish for
9. short, quick sound/dad
10. leader of a country/device used for measuring length

Down

1. container for pouring liquid/baseball player
2. with sudden starts and stops/strips of dried meat
4. unusual/not cooked much
5. say the letters of a word/magical trance
7. student/part of the eye

Homophones 1

A *homophone* is a word that sounds the same as another word but is spelled differently and has a different meaning. Find the homophones of the clues below and place them in the puzzle.

Across

5. reign
7. plain
8. principle
10. peace
11. meet
12. bare
14. mite

Down

1. one
2. band
3. night
4. bale
6. aloud
8. paws
9. beat
10. patience
13. ate

Homophones 2

A *homophone* is a word that sounds the same as another word but is spelled differently and has a different meaning. Find the homophones of the clues below and place them in the puzzle.

Across

2. sun

3. whether

6. hare

7. rowed, rode

9. waist

11. wear, ware

13. steel

14. toad

15. ring

Down

1. flour

2. sail

3. witch

4. through

5. hole

8. way

10. stare

12. herd

13. shone

How Many?

Use the clues below to fill in the puzzle with number words.

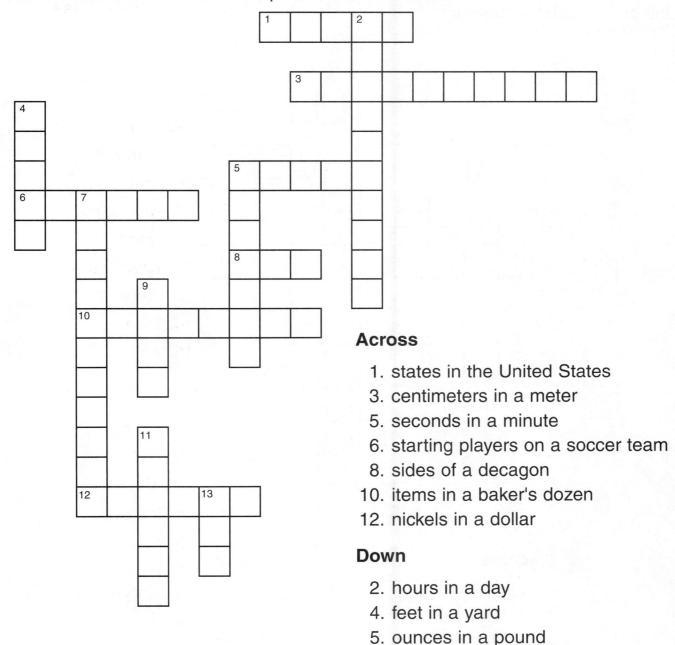

Across

1. states in the United States
3. centimeters in a meter
5. seconds in a minute
6. starting players on a soccer team
8. sides of a decagon
10. items in a baker's dozen
12. nickels in a dollar

Down

2. hours in a day
4. feet in a yard
5. ounces in a pound
7. keys on a piano
9. voices in a quintet
11. inches in a foot
13. decades in a century

How Many Zeros?

How many zeroes are there in each of the numbers named in the clues? Fill in the puzzle with the answers.

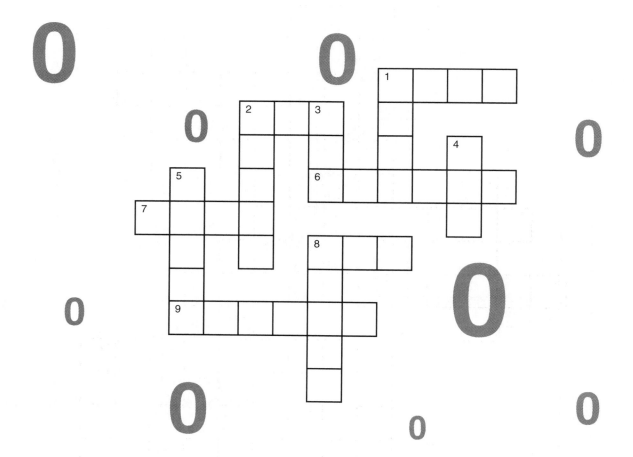

Across

1. ten-thousand
2. hundred
6. hundred-billion
7. billion
8. million
9. trillion

Down

1. hundred-thousand
2. thousand
3. ten
4. ten-billion
5. hundred-million
8. ten million

Irregular Past Tense

Fill in the puzzle with the past-tense forms of the clues given below.

Across

2. begin	10. teach
4. build	11. write
5. stand	12. am
7. freeze	15. think
9. give	16. speak

Down

1. catch	8. throw
3. fly	11. go
4. break	12. weep
5. sleep	13. say
6. drive	14. take

Islands of the World

Which country owns each of islands listed below? Use the Country Box to help you complete the puzzle.

Country Box

Ecuador	United Kingdom	Spain	Japan
Denmark	Greece	United States	Sweden
Canada	Russia	Italy	Portugal
Scotland			Chile

Across

2. Azores
3. Hawaii
4. Gotland
5. Crete
9. Newfoundland
10. Easter
11. Faroe
12. Galapagos

Down

1. Honshu
3. Isle of Man
4. Herbides
6. Franz Josef Land
7. Sicily
8. Canary

It Begins with "Man"

Use the clues below to fill in the puzzle with words that begins with the letters "man."

Across

1. a language spoken in China
2. a tropical fruit
4. a large insect
6. person in charge
7. a small stringed instrument
9. a small book that gives instruction or information
10. to make by hand or machine

Down

1. a large animal that lives in tropical water
3. a shelf above a fire place
4. a famous island in New York
5. a large house
6. a province in Canada
7. numerous
8. a treatment for fingernails

Language Arts

Test your knowledge of language arts—from words to grammar to literature. Fill in the puzzle with the answer to the clues below.

Across

4. Which comes first in a dictionary, "maybe" or "maypole"?
5. subject and _____ make up the two main parts of a sentence
9. punctuation mark used in a contraction
10. If synonym = same, then antonym = _____.
13. punctuation mark between the city and state
14. What two words make up the contraction "won't"?
15. punctuation mark placed after the greeting in a business letter

Down

1. plural of sheep
2. story with a moral at the end
3. rat in *Charlotte's Web*
6. mini dictionary in the back of some textbooks
7. Japanese poetry that follows a pattern of 5-7-5 syllables
8. part of speech that names a person, place, or thing
11. story that is made-up rather than factual
12. statement that tells what a person thinks or believes

Multiplication

Use the clues below to fill in the puzzle with number words.

Across

5. seven times six
9. five times five
10. twelve times ten
11. eight times seven
12. seven times five
13. nine times eleven

Down

1. eleven times five
2. twelve times seven
3. nine times seven
4. five times one
5. six times eight
6. seven times ten
7. nine times nine
8. nine times eight
9. nine times three

Name the Country

Where would you find these famous landmarks? Fill in the puzzle with the names of the countries where these landmarks are located.

Across

2. Great Wall

5. Statue of Liberty

6. Angkor Wat

7. Taj Mahal

8. Effiel Tower

10. Macchu Picchu

Down

1. Parthenon

3. Sydney Opera House

4. Big Ben

7. The Colosseum

9. Sphinx

11. St. Basil's Cathedral

Name Their Sport

Fill in the puzzle with the names of the sports that match these famous athletes.

Babe Ruth

Wayne Gretzky

Across

1. Michelle Kwan
3. Venus Williams
7. Michael Phelps
10. Peyton Manning
11. Evander Holyfield
12. Babe Ruth

Down

2. Dale Ernhardt
4. Pele
5. Lance Armstrong
6. Shaquille O'Neal
8. Tiger Woods
9. Wayne Gretzky

Nicknames

Sometimes, a shorter version or nickname can be substituted for a person's first name. Fill in the puzzle with the matching nicknames of the names below.

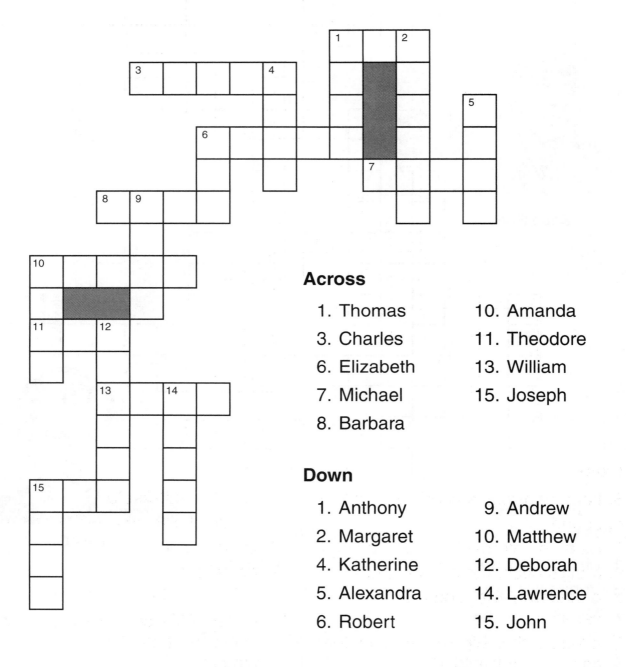

Across

1. Thomas
3. Charles
6. Elizabeth
7. Michael
8. Barbara
10. Amanda
11. Theodore
13. William
15. Joseph

Down

1. Anthony
2. Margaret
4. Katherine
5. Alexandra
6. Robert
9. Andrew
10. Matthew
12. Deborah
14. Lawrence
15. John

"No" Way

Each of the clues below defines a word that has the letters "no" in it. Can you fill in the puzzles with all of the correct "no" words?

Across

3. body part that is used for smelling
4. sound
5. range of information a person has
8. a pig's nose, mouth, and jaws
10. a macaroni-like food made in flat strips
12. a loop with a slip knot that tightens as the rope is pulled
13. wanderer
14. city in Tennessee

Down

1. lengthy written story
2. small, elf-like, imaginary being
6. foolishness
7. no person
9. rap at the door
11. either of the two times each year when day and night are of equal length
12. Biblical man who built an ark

Numbers

Use the clues below to fill in the puzzle with number words.

Across

2. years in a century

4. squares on a checkerboard
   (*Hint: A checkerboard has
   8 rows of 8 squares each.*)

7. horns on a triceratops

10. number in a dozen

11. hours in a day

12. dwarfs in *Snow White*

13. named planets in our
    solar system

Down

1. letters in the English
   alphabet

3. sides on a die

5. sides on a rectangle

6. years in a decade

7. pounds in a ton

8. states in the United States

9. rings of the Olympic symbol

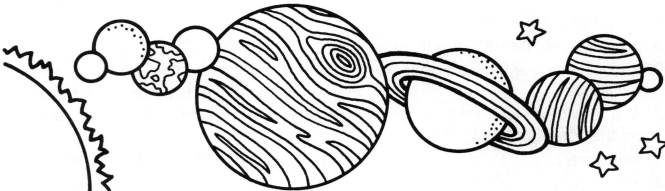

Oxymorons

An *oxymoron* is a figure of speech that combines two words that seem to be opposites. An example is the phrase "pretty ugly." Use the Word Box to complete the oxymorons.

Word Box

shrimp
groom
news
end
wings
live
difference
burn
favorite
adult
luck
full
world

Across

2. old
4. jumbo
5. half
8. same
10. taped
11. freezer
13. front

Down

1. buffalo
3. small
6. bad
7. bride
9. least
12. young

Patterns

Use the clues below to fill in the puzzle with number words.

Across

2. fifteen, twelve, nine, _____

5. twelve, nine, six, three, _____

6. two, five, eight, eleven, _____

9. four, eight, twelve, _____

10. seventeen, thirteen, nine, _____

11. two, four, six, eight, _____

12. three, six, nine, _____

Down

1. one, three, five, seven, _____

3. sixteen, twelve, eight, _____

4. five, ten, fifteen, twenty, _____

6. three, six, nine, twelve, _____

7. five, six, seven, _____

8. seven, eleven, fifteen, _____

Plurals

Fill in the puzzle with the plural forms of the clues given.

Across

2. canary
4. dash
7. address
10. ox
13. ax
14. elf
15. grocery
16. gas
17. fish
18. mattress

Down

1. baby
3. knife
5. scissors
6. valley
8. deer
9. berry
11. battery
12. leaf

Portmanteau Words

Sometimes, the meanings and spellings of two words are combined to create a new word. The combined word is called a *portmanteau* word. Use the Word Box to help you complete the puzzle with portmanteau words.

Word Box				
chortle	fortnight	motel	pixel	splatter
flare	glimmer	motorcross	skylab	squiggle
flurry	moped	paratroops	twirl	telethon

Across

3. motor + cross country
6. gleam + shimmer
8. picture + element
9. sky + laboratory
10. chuckle + snort
11. flutter + hurry
12. fourteen + nights

Down

1. parachute + troops
2. twist + whirl
3. hotel + motor
4. splash + spatter
5. television + marathon
7. motor + pedal
9. squirm + wiggle
11. flame + glare

Proverbs 1

Use the Word Box to help you complete the famous proverbs below.

Word Box

- cake
- chickens
- silver
- pours
- milk
- cat
- join
- mice
- earned
- worm
- gold
- doctor

Across

1. The early bird catches the _____.
3. You can't have your _____ and eat it too.
6. An apple a day keeps the _____ away.
8. Don't count your _____ until they are hatched.
10. It never rains but it _____.
11. A penny saved is a penny _____.

Down

2. Don't cry over spilt _____.
3. Curiosity killed the _____.
4. If you can't beat 'em, _____ 'em.
5. When the cat's away, the _____ will play.
7. Every cloud has a _____ lining.
9. All that glitters is not _____ .

Proverbs 2

Use the Word Box to help you complete the famous proverbs below.

Word Box

friend	thousand
right	waste
leap	heart
sword	better
light	wear
son	fire
choosers	rest

Across

1. Beggars can't be _____.
4. A friend in need is a _____ indeed.
6. Many hands make _____ work.
7. Two heads are _____ than one.
9. Like father, like _____ .
10. This is the first day of the _____ of your life.
11. Haste makes _____ .

12. Look before you _____ .

Down

2. The pen is mightier than the _____.
3. Absence makes the _____ grow fonder.
5. Where there's smoke, there's _____.
8. A picture is worth a _____ words.
10. Two wrongs don't make a _____.
11. If the shoe fits, _____ it.

Rhyme Time

Each clue below describes two words that rhyme. (For example, "tiny shopping center" could be "small mall.")

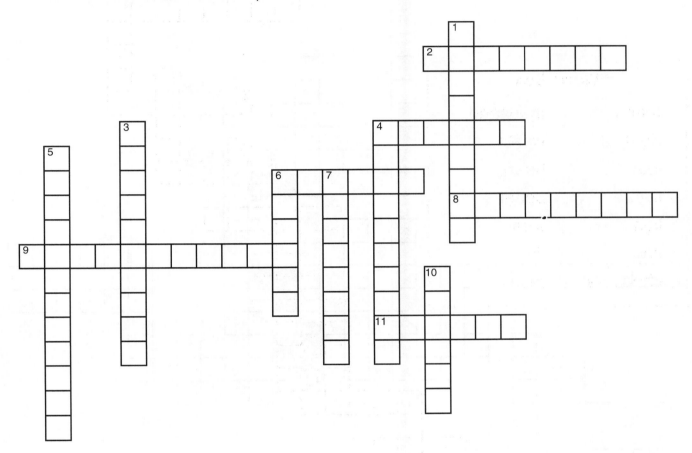

Across

2. kind grizzly
4. unhappy father
6. large swine
8. extra horse
9. dog kiss
11. feline pad

Down

1. loafing flower
3. rodent home
4. smooth hen
5. calm man
6. beetle embrace
7. purple gorilla
10. overweight kitty

Roman Numerals

Fill in the puzzle with the number words the Roman numerals stand for.

Across

3. LX
4. XVIII
6. X
9. L
10. XII
11. C
14. XI
15. XVII
18. XIII
19. LXX
20. IV
21. II
22. V

Down

1. XIV
2. XXX
5. XC
7. XV
8. XVI
9. XL
10. XX
12. VIII
13. VII
16. LXXX
17. I
18. III

Scrambled Math

Unscramble the clues below to complete the puzzle with math words.

Across

3. roze
4. dad
8. tipmulyl
9. simet
10. geanevit

12. viddie
13. slup
14. trasucbt
15. sinum

Down

1. tracifon
2. citsaamthem
5. gidit
6. bumner

7. lafh
11. nitodida
14. mus

Season Scramble

Unscramble the clues below to complete the puzzle with words about the seasons of the year.

Across

3. aeknlosfw
5. oht
6. twiren
8. msremu
10. nus
12. anosmwn

Down

1. signrp
2. seleav
4. rseoflw
7. atnmuu
9. nrai
11. iwdn

Similes

A *simile* is a way to compare two things. Complete the similes below and fill in the puzzle. Use the Word Box to help you.

Word Box

thunder	day	stars	eel	bird	silk
feather	wink	ice	glove	pig	mule
button	pancake	honey	bee	dogs	glass

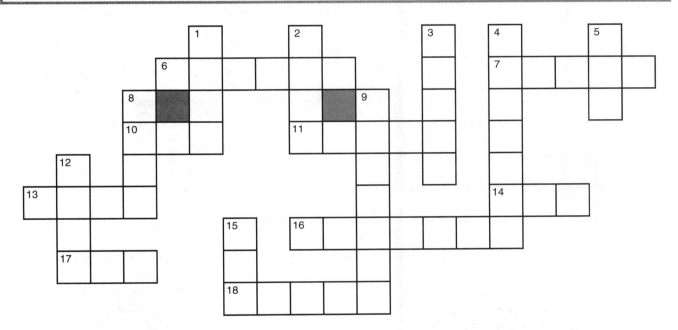

Across

6. as cute as a _____
7. as sweet as _____
10. as cold as _____
11. eyes like _____
13. as soft as _____
14. as slippery as an _____
16. as light as a _____
17. as clear as _____
18. fits like a _____

Down

1. as stubborn as a _____
2. fought like cats and _____
3. as smooth as _____
4. as loud as _____
5. as busy as a _____
8. as quick as a _____
9. as flat as a _____
12. sing like a _____
15. eats like a _____

Sports Scrambles

Unscramble the clues below to complete the puzzle with sports words.

Across

2. flog
5. laooflbt
7. abbselal
9. asblbtekla

12. gnikis
13. gurnnin
14. miwsimgn

Down

1. ockeyh
3. lelolalbvy
4. lsofalbt
6. sitnen
7. glyccibin

8. glterwins
10. ybgur
11. crosce
12. taksgni

Subtraction

Use the clues below to fill in the puzzle with number words.

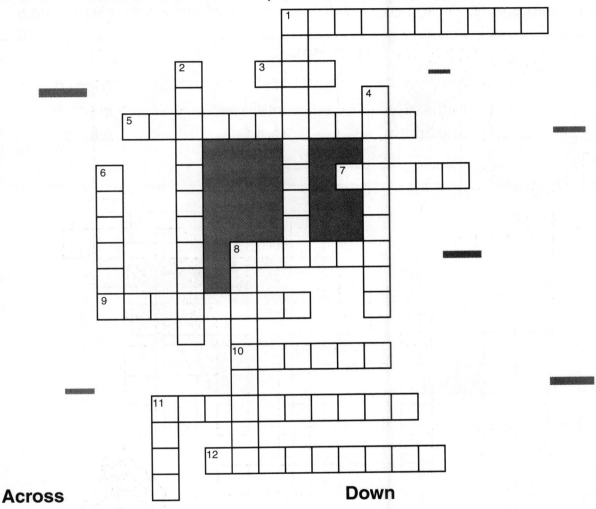

Across

1. thirty-four minus ten
3. eighteen minus five minus seven
5. forty minus seventeen
7. thirty minus eight minus fifteen
8. forty-two minus eleven minus nineteen
9. forty-four minus twenty-five
10. fifty-one minus twenty-one
11. sixty minus twelve
12. fifty-five minus eleven

Down

1. fifty minus fifteen
2. thirty-nine minus twelve
4. thirty-three minus sixteen
6. twenty minus nine
8. forty minus eighteen
11. twenty-six minus twenty minus two

49

Synonyms

A *synonym* is a word that has the same meaning as another word. Use the Word Box to help you fill in the puzzle with synonyms of the words given below.

Word Box			
ancient	brief	feeble	rugged
ask	comical	intelligent	slender
awful	enormous	rapid	whole
awkward			

Across

1. uncomfortable
6. fast
7. huge
8. smart
10. thin
11. terrible

Down

1. question
2. old
3. weak
4. entire
5. funny
6. strong, tough
9. short

The Other Half

Complete the clues below with the missing half of the pair. Fill in the puzzle.

Across

1. pencil and _____
3. macaroni and _____
6. pins and _____
10. meat and _____
12. nuts and _____
13. song and _____

Down

2. left and _____
4. safe and _____
5. soap and _____
7. bacon and _____
8. lost and _____
9. sticks and _____
11. now and _____
14. tooth and _____

The Zodiac

Use the Word Box to help you match the sign of the Zodiac with the symbol that represents it. Fill in the puzzle with the signs of the Zodiac.

Word Box

Aries	Leo	Sagittarius
Taurus	Virgo	Capricorn
Gemini	Libra	Aquarius
Cancer	Scorpio	Pisces

Across

2. bull
7. lion
9. twins
10. balance
11. goat
12. archer

Down

1. maiden
3. ram
4. scorpion
5. crab
6. water bearer
8. fish

Where Are These Bones?

In what part of the body is each of these bones found?

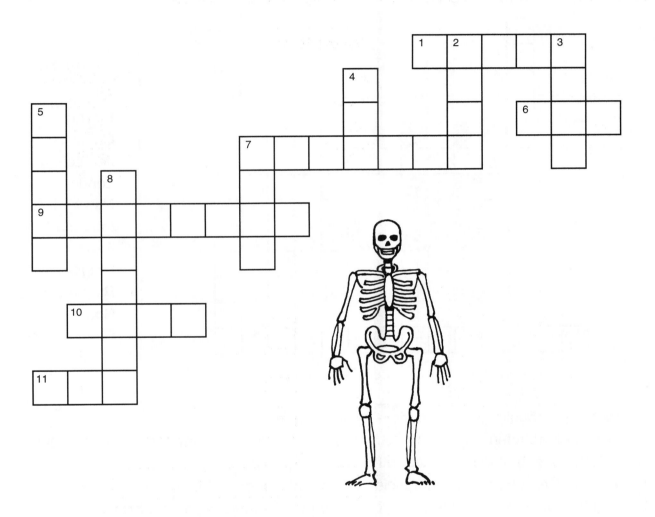

Across

1. femur
6. mandible
7. phalanges
9. clavicle
10. vertebrae
11. humerus

Down

2. pelvis
3. cranium
4. tibia
5. ribs
7. metatarsal
8. ulna

       #5997 Start to Finish: Crossword Puzzles

Which City Are You Visiting?

Use the City Box and the clues below to fill in the puzzle with the names of popular tourist destinations.

City Box

Athens
Beijing
Cairo
Jerusalem
London
New York City
Panama City
Paris
Prague
Rio de Janeiro
Rome
San Francisco

Across

3. visit the Acropolis; 2004 Summer Olympics were here
5. visit the Forbidden City and the Great Wall; will host the Summer Olympics in 2008
9. visit the beach of Ipanema; go to the Carnival parade
10. visit the Great Pyramids and ancient ruins; sail along the Nile River
11. visit the rain forest; take a ride through the most famous canal on Earth

Down

1. visit the Effiel Tower; known as the "City of Lights"
2. visit the Buckingham Palace; ride a double-decker bus or the huge Ferris wheel
4. visit the Transamerican Tower; ride across the Golden Gate bridge or on a cable car
6. visit the Castle; capital of the Czech Republic; called "the city of 100 spires"
7. visit the Statue of Liberty and Empire State Building; go to see a play or musical on Broadway
8. visit the Wailing Wall; home to three of the world's religions: Judaism, Christianity, Islam
9. visit the Colosseum; explore the ancient forum

Words That Tell the Number

Which numbers match the clues below? Fill in the puzzle with the answers.

Across

3. megabyte, megapixel

4. triangle, trio

5. bicycle, binocular

7. centipede, century

10. gigabyte, gigawatt

12. decade, decible, decimal

Down

1. pentagon, pentahlon

2. quadrangle, quadruplet

4. kilogram, kilometer

6. heptathlon, septuplet

8. hexagon, sextuplet

9. octave, octopus

11. unicorn, monorail, unicycle

Answer Key

Page 4

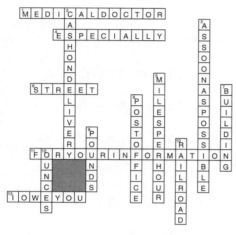

Page 5

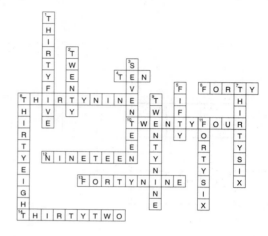

Page 6

Page 7

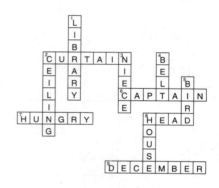

Page 8

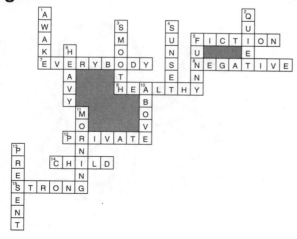

Page 9

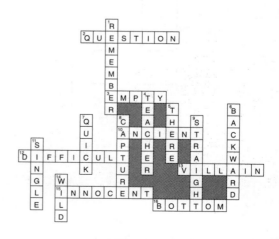

Answer Key *(cont.)*

Page 10

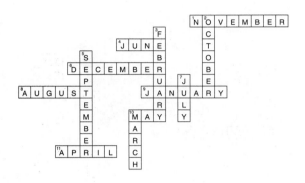

Page 11

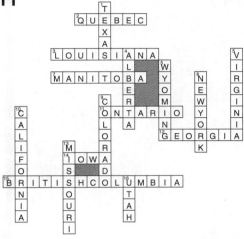

Page 12

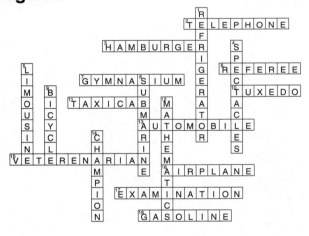

Page 13

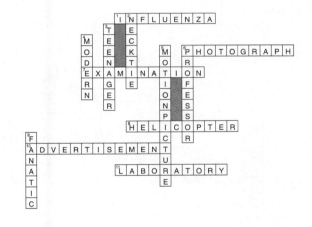

Page 14

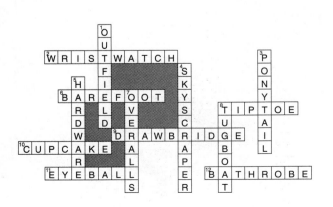

Page 15

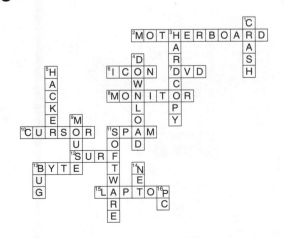

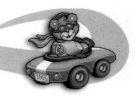

Answer Key *(cont.)*

Page 16

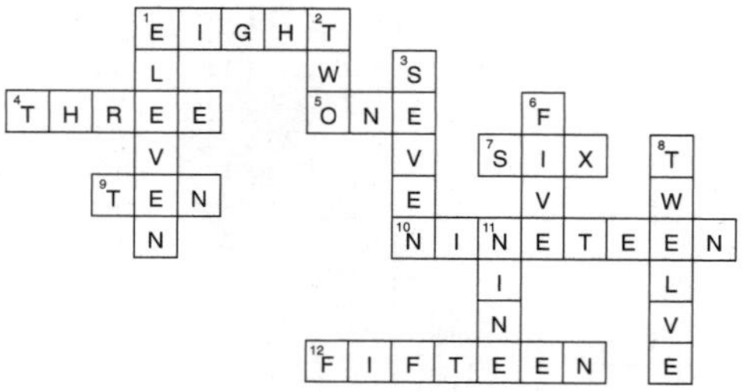

Page 17

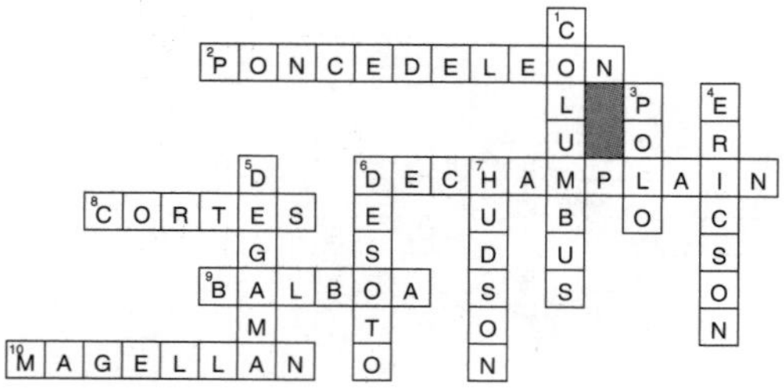

Page 18

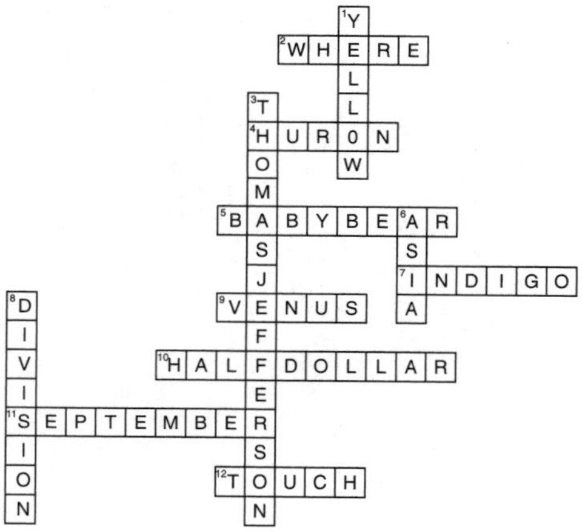

Page 19

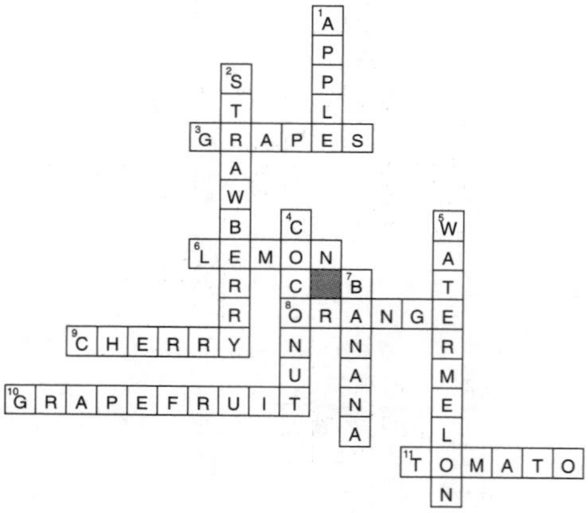

Page 20

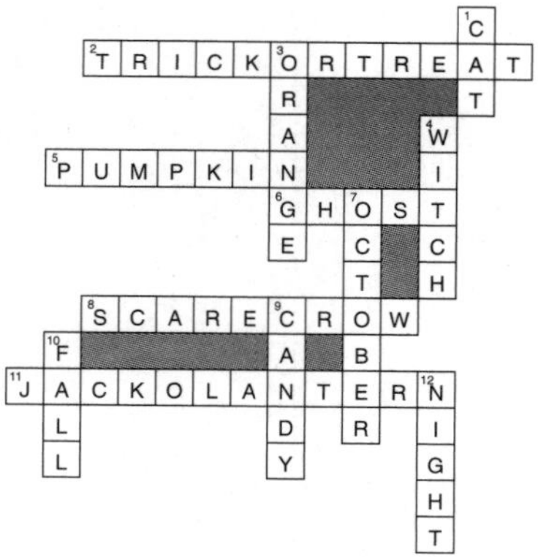

Page 21

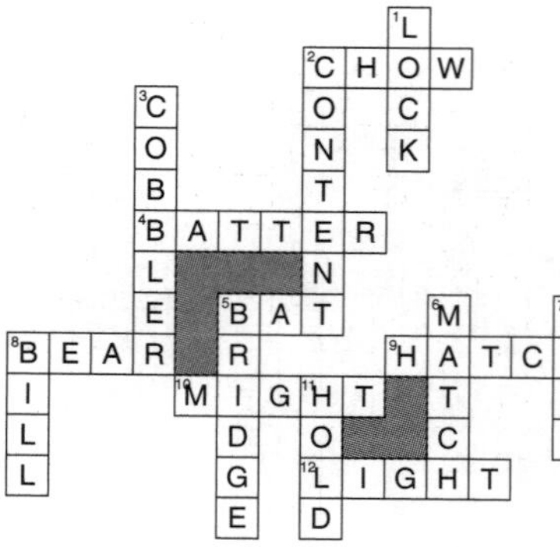

Answer Key *(cont.)*

Page 22

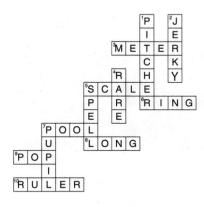

Page 23

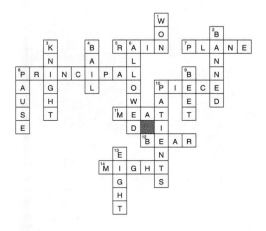

Page 24

Page 25

Page 26

Page 27

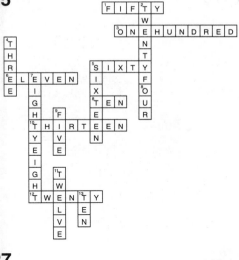

Answer Key *(cont.)*

Page 28

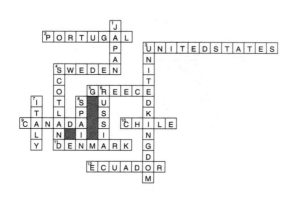

Page 29

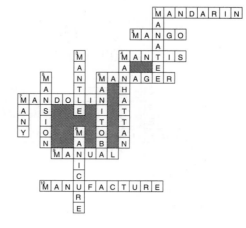

Page 30

Page 31

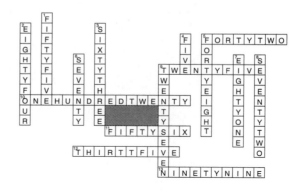

Page 32

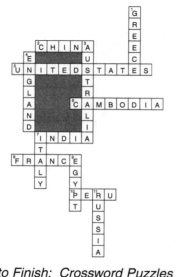

Page 33

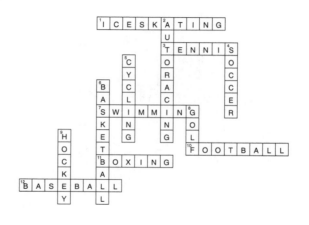

Answer Key *(cont.)*

Page 34

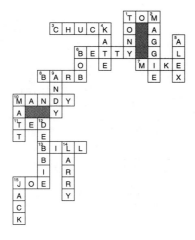

Page 35

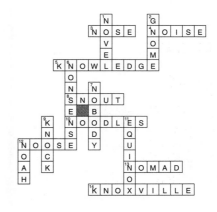

Page 36

Page 37

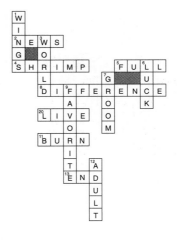

Page 38

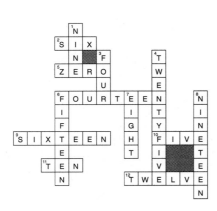

Page 39

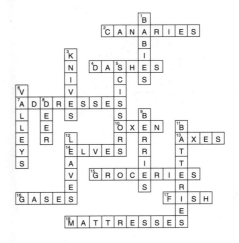

©Teacher Created Resources, Inc.

61

#5997 Start to Finish: Crossword Puzzles

Answer Key *(cont.)*

Page 40

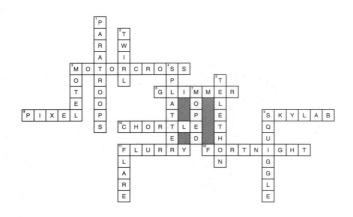

Page 41

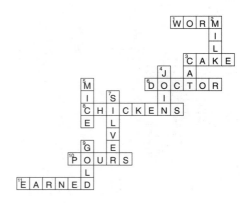

Page 42

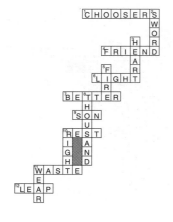

Page 43

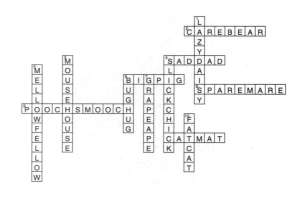

Page 44

Page 45

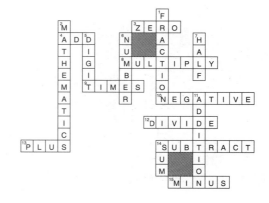

Answer Key *(cont.)*

Page 46

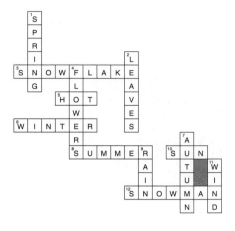

Page 47

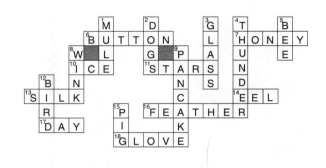

Page 48

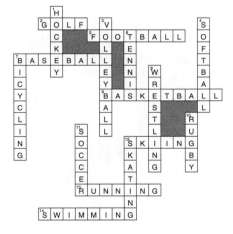

Page 49

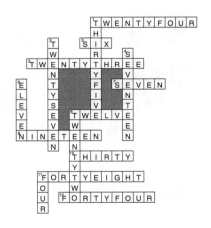

Page 50

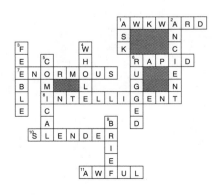

Page 51

Answer Key (cont.)

Page 52

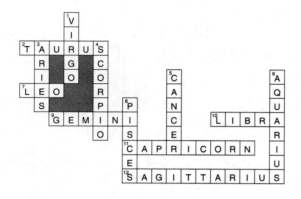

Page 53

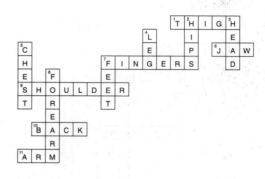

Page 54

Page 55